The Land Where I Live

Written by Mary-Anne Creasy
Series Consultant: Linda Hoyt

WorldWise
Content-based Learning

Contents

Introduction

Antonia, Jackson and Daniela all live in different parts of the world, with very different climates.

What are their houses like? How do they get to school? What games do they play? What sort of food do they eat?

Everything that they do is affected by the climate of the place where they live.

Chapter 1

Between the mountains and the sea

Antonia stops her horse under a stringy bark tree. The hot sunlight pierces the shade. She pulls a water bottle from her saddlebag and takes a long drink, swishing the water around her dry mouth. A sudden stiff breeze rustles the limp gum leaves above her head. She looks up through the branches. The canopy of the forest sways violently in the wind. Black ash flutters across the dense blue sky. She sniffs the air – smoke! Quickly, she nudges her horse through scrubby bushes and out into the open grassy paddock. She leans forward, urging him to gallop towards the house ahead. Her mother waves and calls to her. It's a bushfire, and they need to get out.

My name is Antonia, and I live near Queanbeyan in New South Wales, Australia. I love living here as we have dry weather with blue skies for most of the year. I can ride my horse almost every day after school. The other reason I like living here is we are only three hours from the coast and three hours from the mountains. In summer we like to go to the beach, and in winter we can drive to the Snowy Mountains to go skiing.

Temperate climate

Queanbeyan is in southeastern New South Wales. It has a temperate climate, with warm to hot dry summers, short cool winters, and a wet spring when most of the rain falls. Because of the hot dry weather in summer, there is a danger of bushfires.

The danger of bushfires

The only thing I don't like about living here is the danger of bushfires. We live outside the town on dry grassy land, near a forest reserve. Our home is in a high-risk area for bushfires. Even in winter we can get bushfires. Sometimes the fire department visits to check that we have made our house and sheds safe. They make sure we don't let trees grow near buildings and keep the grass short. They remind us to clear our gutters of dead leaves.

One summer, it was very hot and dry and the wind started to blow. We had warnings all the time about the dangers of bushfires. No one was allowed to light barbecues or use a lawnmower, because just one spark could start a fire. Then we saw a bushfire in the distance coming towards us. We had to leave our house quickly. We took our two horses and our dogs with us.

We had to stay away until the fire was put out and it was safe to return. When we came back, our house was burned down, and some of the paddocks and fences too. We had to live at my grandparents' house until we could rebuild our house.

Coming from Italy

My grandfather **migrate**d from Italy to Australia when he was only 19 because the government needed people to work on a big construction project, the Snowy Mountains Scheme. Thousands of people came from Europe to work on this project. He got a job as a carpenter. After two years he got a job working for a furniture company making cabinets. People liked his work, but he wanted to make his own designs, so after a few years he decided to start his own business. His brother came over from Italy and together they bought a factory and employed other people to help them make lots of different furniture.

Eating and growing things

Because my family has an Italian background, we often like to eat Italian food. Italian food uses things like tomatoes, capsicums, zucchinis, garlic and olives. We grow some of the fruit and vegetables we eat. The climate here is a lot like Italy's climate. We have warm dry summers and colder winters so it's good for growing fruit and vegetables. We grow tomatoes, eggplants, zucchinis, peppers and grapes. We also have olive, apricot and lemon trees.

Our dry climate means that sometimes there is not enough water for our crops. We have to bring water from rivers that are far away. Lemon and apricot trees need a lot of water. For a few years there has not been enough water in the rivers, so we have had to let some of our fruit trees die. My mum thinks we should start growing native Australian plants, which don't need much water.

Did you know?
Some Italian families get together at the end of summer to cook huge pots of tomato sauce flavoured with herbs and onions. They bring all the tomatoes they have grown. They put the sauce into jars, so they can have a delicious homemade tomato *sugo* all winter.

Chapter 2

Living at the top of the world

*It is dark, freezing, and so cold that it is dangerous to be outside. You can hardly see Jackson's face hidden inside the hood of his fur-lined coat. His clothes are warm and thick. His mother has the car's engine running and she drives him the short distance to school. This is winter in a **polar** climate.*

My name is Jackson, and I live in Utqiaġvik (say *oot – kay-ahg – vik*), Alaska, in the United States. I love living here. I am proud that our town is the most northerly town in the United States. People who come here say it's cold – and I guess it is, but we are used to it.

Utqiaġvik is in the Arctic region, near the North Pole. The town is located in a **polar desert**. This means it doesn't get much rain, and it is cold all the time.

❄ Polar climates

Polar climates are found in regions near the very top and the very bottom of the earth. For two months in winter, it is dark all day and night. In some places, the ground is frozen year-round, making it impossible to grow food.

In the summer, the sun does not set for three months. It is always daylight. The summer is short and the climate never gets really warm.

11

My Arctic town

Utqiaġvik is far away from other places and hard to get to. You can get here only by plane, except in the summer when there is also a boat service. In the winter, the ocean freezes. In the summer, all the town's big supplies, like building materials, machinery and cars, are brought in by boat.

The area around Utqiaġvik has a lot of oil and **natural gas**. My home and all the other buildings are heated by gas from the nearby gas fields.

All the town's buildings are on **stilts**. This is because the ground is frozen, and the warmth from the heated buildings would make the icy ground melt and become soggy. The buildings would collapse.

A cargo ship on the ice

Most homes have pipes that bring in water and take away waste. The town has a special underground tunnel that is **insulated** from the cold. The pipes run through this tunnel. This stops the water and waste in the pipes from freezing.

Our summer would feel cold to most people. In Utqiaġvik, we are so used to the cold that I sometimes wear a T-shirt outside when it's only 4 degrees Celsius. But we still heat our house in summer because it's nice to come in to a warm house.

The jawbones of a whale form an arch to the Arctic Ocean.

Did you know?
Fresh food is expensive in Utqiaġvik because everything has to be brought in by plane. Food can't be grown because the ground is frozen.

13

Getting around

Mum takes my brother and me to school on her way to work. But the other day our car wouldn't start, so we caught a taxi. Taxis are very cheap because people who don't have a car need to use them all the time. There is also a school bus that picks up children around the town. We don't walk to school because we don't have footpaths. Roads and footpaths can't be paved because in summer, the top layer of the ground melts. Paved footpaths and roads would crack and sink.

Having fun

The first snow usually falls in October. It snows until spring and there is always snow on the ground until the summer. Sometimes on the weekend, my cousin takes my brother and me for rides on his **snowmobile**.

In the winter it is cold and dark all the time, so we can't play outside. We spend a lot of time indoors. But that doesn't stop us from having fun.

At home, we have TV and computer games. At my school we have two indoor playgrounds, a rock-climbing wall and a big gymnasium where we can practise basketball or play games.

Our town has a heated swimming pool and an ice-skating rink. My cousins play ice hockey. When I'm older, I want to play, too.

 **Did you know?**

Independence Day is a big celebration in Utqiaġvik. There is a Fourth of July parade and lots of food. After that, there are games and contests like blanket tossing and seal boat racing, followed by traditional dances to drum music.

On New Year's Day in January, when it's dark all the time, there are fireworks in the middle of the day.

15

Chapter 3

The rainforest, my home

Equator

*Daniela walks along a muddy path through the rainforest. She is careful not to brush past the vines carrying a line of huge ants. The air is alive with the sounds of insects and frogs. High above the thick **canopy** of trees, a flock of parrots screech. She peers through the leaves. Are those monkeys sitting in the tree? **Perspiration** runs down her cheek; the air is heavy with moisture. In the distance there is a rumble of thunder. The heavy rain will come soon, as it does almost every day. She walks quickly along the path. Fat drops of rain splatter onto her face. Time to go home.*

My name is Daniela, and I live in Ecuador, South America. Ecuador is a country on the equator. I live near a river in the Amazon Rainforest. We have a tropical climate. It is never extremely hot or extremely cold here, but it does rain a lot. Sometimes the river rises and floods villages and homes.

 Did you know?

The equator divides the earth into the northern and southern hemispheres.

16

Climates at the equator

Most areas that lie on or near the equator have a climate that is always warm. There are few changes in temperature throughout the day and night. The sun rises and sets at about the same time every day of the year.

A village on stilts

I live with my mother and two older brothers in a small timber house in our village. My brothers work with my father, who goes into the forest and cuts down trees. They sell the timber to other families for their houses. My mother, aunt and grandma grow vegetables, which they sell at the market in a nearby town.

Our houses are made of wood and are on **stilts**. The stilts keep us off the wet ground and away from rainforest animals that might want to come inside. We have a big covered platform at the back of our house where we sit when it rains. There are big windows, but they don't have glass in them because it doesn't get cold and we like the air coming through our houses. Most houses have roofs that are covered in dried grass. The grass helps **muffle** the sound of the heavy rain falling on the roof.

Eating

We learn to hunt and fish in the forest. My brothers and I like to fish for piranha, but we have to be careful when we take out the hook, because they have very sharp teeth!

If we want a snack, we can find almost anything we want to eat in the forest. Because it rains so much, plants and trees are always growing and some have fruit. My favourite fruits are bananas and guavas.

Getting around

We live on the river, and our school is further away in another village. There are no roads going to my school, so we travel up the river in a canoe. I love to swim in the river when it is hot, but yesterday I went swimming and I saw a snake in the water, so I got out quickly!

Getting dressed and getting wet

Because the temperature is always the same, I can dress the same way every day. When I go to school, I wear a white T-shirt with a black skirt or pants with socks and sneakers. I don't have to worry about taking a jacket because I know it won't get cold.

When I was younger, it got really cold for a week. It is usually about 30 degrees Celsius during the day, but that week it was only 20 degrees Celsius, and even a bit colder at night. It was weird and not very nice. My father made a fire on the ground outside to warm us until bedtime, and I wore all my clothes because I was not used to the cold. I don't think I would want to live in a cold climate.

Sometimes it rains when we are in the canoe going to school or coming home. But we are used to that because it rains nearly every day. There are pieces of plastic for us to put over our heads, and some kids have umbrellas. But if it's not raining heavily, it doesn't matter because the rain is nice and cool.

Ecuador

Amazon
Rainforest

SOUTH
AMERICA

Conclusion

No climate is perfect. There are good things and bad things no matter where you live in the world. Even a warm, comfortable climate can have seasonal floods or bushfires, which people get used to and prepare for.

Humans are good at **adapting** to the climate in which they live. That is why we can survive in so many different places in the world.

Glossary

adapting   changing to suit a place or situation

canopy   the highest layer of branches in a forest

insulated   to have added material to something to keep cold out and heat in

migrated   to have moved from one place to another

muffle   to deaden the sound

native   from a particular place

natural gas   gas taken from under the ground and used as fuel

perspiration   sweat

polar   relating to the area near the North or South Pole

polar desert   a polar region with less than 25 centimetres of rainfall during the warmest months

snowmobile   a vehicle used for travelling on snow or ice

stilts   posts that support a building above the ground

Index